tea time with the reaper

a true story of love, life and lessons learned

by d.mccormick

ISBN: 978-1-72-024174-4

for babydoll

9

"that's joe"

those were the first words i ever spoke to her.

and that ridiculous 'pick up line' was as improbable as our meeting.

Angela was exhausted having just returned from cincinnati from yet another nine inch nails concert and had every intention of staying home that night to cuddle with her cat yoriko. i, as a non-drinker and vegan (at the time) had zero business hanging out at a venice beach dive bar renowned for its hamburgers.

yet, whether it was chance, fate, or simply the random insistence of our respective acquaintances, our paths crossed at hinanos on friday, august twenty-second, 2008.

those first two words lead to us chatting throughout the night, in between her checking on her friends and us being thoroughly amused by joe's antics and solid pool playing skills despite the number of drinks he had enjoyed. our conversation quickly bypassed the standard first-meeting small-talk and evolved into discussing real stuff; the difference between a true friend and a friendly acquaintance, family and relatives, needing and wanting, and how we had both come to a point in our lives where we did

not need anyone to feel complete or fulfilled.

all told, it was the most enjoyable, honest and surprisingly easiest

conversation i had ever had in my life.

usually at this point in the story people always want to know,

"did you ask for her number?"

my answer, "nope."

it was my belief that if she had enjoyed our conversation as much as i

had, and wished to continue it at a later date, she would let me know.

as both of our groups began to leave the bar, i watched Angela tend to

someone who was a little 'worse for wear'. in that moment i had my first

glimpse into the kind of person she truly was. that insight was then quickly

surpassed when she walked over to me and asked,

"do you want my number?"

"absolutely!"

after a few texts back and forth that night and over the following days,

we agreed to a date that coming thursday. i suggested that we visit the

'bodies' exhibition which was on display at the california science center in

los angeles. for those unfamiliar with 'bodies', this is a display of

plastinated specimens (human bodies that have been preserved in plastic)

which are presented in varying of degrees of dissection and life-like

positions so that you are able to experience and view the body's organs,

tissues and systems in a very intimate and unique way.

a lot of people are shocked to hear that i suggested taking this girl, whom i had just met, to look at something so graphic on our first date. personally i thought it was the perfect litmus test; if she could appreciate dead bodies, she could appreciate me.

Angela and i met outside the science center and i can still remember her walking up in her jeans and black cardigan. yes she looked really good, but it wasn't her appearance that struck me the most. it was her energy, her swagger, which i can best describe as a gorgeous smile, long flowing hair, with her two middle fingers in the air.

we walked around the exhibit for about an hour or so, speaking only briefly as we looked at the various real-life 'exploded diagrams'. once we were done, we strolled around the neighboring exposition park and los angeles coliseum grounds chatting about anything and everything. from there, we decided that we should grab a bite in westwood where our conversation continued to flow for the next fews hours as we shared our individual backstories.

we spoke of our divorces, our lives growing up, her mother's death when Angela was a teenager, my mother's illness, music, sports, places we had been and places we wanted to go.

identical to our first meeting, neither of us held anything back and nothing was off limits. and with each passing moment, Angela's true beauty continued to grow.

as we both had work the following day, we reluctantly decided to call it a night. i walked her to her car, and what happened next is something that she would always remind me of for years to come;

i gave her a hug goodnight.

not a kiss.

a hug.

in my defense, i was so enamored with her that i did not want to risk offending her by being too forward, or worse, give her a lack-luster first kiss. so i thought a hug was a good idea.

apparently Angela did not.

i would eventually come to learn that she interpreted this as a 'we're just going to be friends' gesture and a definitive sign that there would be no second date.

well, she was wrong.

we did have a second date two days later.

and that date never ended.

for all intents and purposes i moved in that saturday night. i almost always slept at her apartment, rarely returning to my own place in venice other than for a quick pit stop in-between the gym, work and returning back 'home' to be with Angela.

understandably this 'fast track' approach concerned many of Angela's inner circle. they were very apprehensive about her moving so fast with someone that she had 'just met', 'barely knew' and that none of them had even spoken to yet.

to them, our relationship sounded more like a modern day fairy tale, urban myth or nightmare in the making than actual reality.

little did they know.

ſ ꓱ

over the coming weeks we spent nearly every spare moment together as she showed me around her city of angels. events, museums, restaurants, iconic sights - it was fantastic. too many 'first-times' to count, all spent with this incredible woman who was a virtual encyclopedia on everything she spoke of and who relished in sharing them all with me. Angela knew los angeles as if she was a part of it, or more accurately, it a part of her.

one of our favorite places to go early on in our relationship was zuma beach. more of a locals-only spot, zuma is located a few miles north on the pacific coast highway (or 'pch' to the locals) just past malibu. it is a nice quiet place to sit on the beach and watch the sun set. it was during one of our visits that Angela informed me that she was going to las vegas in a few weeks for another nine inch nails show, but that i wasn't allowed to go with her.

"why not?" i asked

"because you would try to marry me"

we both had a good laugh and began bantering about what our perfect vegas wedding would include; we would both have to be dressed all in black, it would have to take place in a cheesy yet cute little chapel, and no one need be in attendance except for the king himself.

now whether she was only playing around or using a little reverse psychology, a few weeks later and just over nine weeks after first meeting her, i found myself on one knee asking Angela to be my wife.

the most memorable part of the proposal wasn't what i said, but how long it took.

we were on the top balcony of the getty center museum overlooking its central gardens, much of the city's westside and the pacific ocean. i was building up the courage to tell Angela how lucky i was to have met her, how much she meant to me and how i could not imagine the rest of my life without her, when an older asian lady began belting out what i can only describe as chinese opera.

it was like being trapped in a comedy sketch.

each and every time i began to open my mouth and speak, this little old lady would start signing at full volume. again and again. chorus after chorus. even as the sun began to set and the temperature dropping, there seemed to be no foreseeable end in sight to her performance. i was beginning to think i would have to plan another time to 'pop the question'.

luckily, and thankfully, our serenade came to a close and i was finally able to ask the most incredible woman i had ever met if she would honor me by coming my wife.

she said "yes"

to recap;

we met august twenty-second

we moved in together on august thirtieth

we were engaged on october twenty-fifth

and then married on december fourteenth . . . in las vegas . . . by elvis

by all conventional standards, the odds of that timeline actually happening in real-life are slim to none. and even if it did happen, the odds of that relationship surviving are even less. what do you think the odds are of the people in that relationship never fighting?

no arguments.

no bickering.

no name calling.

ever.

Angela and i proved that urban myths can come true.

and we did it effortlessly.

from the beginning we were completely open and honest

our first picture together

september 2008

.

8

anyone who met Angela knew that she was a force of nature.

beautiful.

caring.

strong.

undeniable.

whether personally or professionally, she applied a philosophy to everything much like that of horace's famous 'carpe diem'. except with Angela, it was a bit more specific;

"i want what i want when i want it".

it was this fierce approach to life that helped her fulfill her childhood dream of becoming a fashion designer. of moving to california. indulging her love of art, food and wine. spending time with the 'family' that she built from scratch. traveling and experiencing different parts of the world. and yes, enjoying as many 'head banging' concerts as she could.

Angela's desire to experience life in the way she wanted was equally matched by her drive to succeed professionally. how else can you explain someone moving to one of the most competitive cities in the world with no job or place to live secured, go from making cappuccinos at the neighborhood coffee shop to eventually becoming an executive at one of the most prominent and well respected post-production facilities in the world.

regardless of the environment she was in, Angela's ability to accomplish a task and exceed expectations, all while successfully managing the chaos of budgets, deadlines and unimaginable personalities was a sight to behold.

and in addition to her drive, she had a secret to being successful;

she busted her ass.

and . . . then she rewarded herself.

alma, bayless, big deans, blais, boston, bourdain, broad, chicago, chanel, cocktails, colicchio, conant, conservatory, disney, dodgers, dior, drag, foo fighters, getty, hawaii, hinanos, lacma, lakers, las vegas, london, malaysia, maya, moca, new york city, nin, palm desert, palm springs, patriots, portugal, prada, puscifer, ramsay, ru paul, samuelson, san francisco, santa barbara, santos, seasmoke, scotland, singapore, stella, tool, usta, voltaggio. and that is just a few of her favorite experiences that does not include any of her favorite architects, artists, film makers, movies, photographers, writers, etc.

Angela's interests were vast.

she always knew what she wanted.

what she needed to do to earn it.

and then she made it happen.

whether it was a concert out of town, spontaneous drinks with the girls, or her annual trip to palm springs, Angela did what she wanted, when she wanted it. and she never needed to ask for anyone's permission. nor forgiveness. she worked hard and deserved to play hard.

and i was happily along for the ride.

on the very rare occasion when Angela might hesitate as to whether or not to buy those 'cute six inch heels', make a reservation at the newest restaurant or plan another getaway, i would simply recite her mantra;

"i want what i want when i want it".

it was the undeniable reminder that the result of not 'going for it' always yielded one of life's worst outcomes; regret.

we knew who we were and what we wanted

babydoll, the king and i

december 2008

7

for the next seven years, we were 'that couple'.

the couple who enjoyed spending time with each other more than with anyone else. the couple who left each other cute, random notes. the couple who never let a day, or even a few hours pass without telling each other "i love you."

and much like most couples, we spent time discussing our long term dreams and how we planned to make them happen.

while Angela dreamt of fashion design as a child, she was drawn to wine as an adult.

like many, she was a fan of its taste but it was the entire process that excited her. everything from the history of the vines, the conditions of the soil, the weather that the grapes were exposed to as they grew, the harvest, fermentation, bottling, aging. she loved all of the deceivingly minute details that play such vital roles in the wine's journey to its final expression.

now, for those who may have found the above paragraph 'a little much' or 'overly dramatic', do yourself a favor and watch two of Angela's favorite films; the documentary 'blood into wine' and the movie 'sideways'. if after those two films you do not have a greater appreciation for the artistry, difficulty and sheer magic that goes into crafting a quality wine, nothing will (and that is coming from someone who does not even drink).

one of the many benefits of living in los angeles is its proximity to world class wine regions, which allowed Angela and i to enjoy frequent day trips or weekend getaways to tasting rooms and wineries throughout southern and central california. one of our favorite areas to visit was the santa ynez valley.

we would hop in the car early on a sunday before the brunch crowd was even awake, drive the one hundred and fifty miles north to find ourselves magically transported to a completely different world. rolling hills, endless vineyards and charming little towns. and whether it was with tasting room staff, other winery visitors or the actual winemakers, she loved talking about wine.

Angela was truly in her element.

after a day spent driving around enjoying a tasting or three, we would usually find ourselves at one of the incredible local restaurants enjoying fantastic food and chatting about our day. recalling the cute winery cats and dogs we had met, her new favorite bottle of wine (of which a few cases may have found their way into the trunk of her car) as well as what it would be like to live in the area.

both Angela and i thought that wine country would be a fantastic place to 'retire' to once we were ready to say 'goodbye' to the monster known as los angeles.

in the summer of 2015, it said goodbye to us.

ᚠ ᛗ

during the first part of that year, we had been actively trying to purchase a home and as any local angeleno will attest, the los angeles real estate market is far from 'buyer friendly'. inflexible sellers, limited inventory and ludicrous prices make a normally challenging process overwhelmingly difficult and stressful.

it was during the inspection process of yet another property that Angela turned to me and said, "if this one doesn't happen, it's a sign for us to pull the plug and move to wine country."

my reply, "done!"

and true to form of our entire house buying experience, the owners were unwilling to negotiate on the expensive, lengthy and previously undisclosed list of deficiencies.

so the decision was made.

it was time to 'escape from la'.

our plan was to extend our apartment lease in downtown los angeles to the following summer, allowing us a little more than a year to thoroughly investigate central california and decide on where would be best to live. we would visit all of the little cities and towns, confirm what the rental options were and gain a better overall feel for the vibe of each area.

plus a summer time move would be a perfect follow up to our annual spring-time tradition; traveling out of town for Angela's birthday.

although these trips were meant to celebrate her, while we experienced someplace new, Angela had a very 'scientific' reason behind them. according to her, "if you're out of town on your birthday you don't age."

the first few birthday trips we took were in the usa but they eventually expanded overseas. for 2016, our destination was scotland. we were both super excited as neither of us had ever been before, and being the incredible producer she was, Angela had a wonderful itinerary planned which included a ton of amazing restaurants and local sights to experience.

with scotland being our last trip prior to leaving los angeles, followed by our move north later that summer, the first few weeks of the year were hectic with a lot of planning and tying up of loose ends. for Angela that included a trip to the doctor at the beginning of february.

which lead to the phone call.

the call that no one ever wants to receive.

"they found something."

we knew what those words meant

rain room at lacma

february 2016

6

Angela was referred to the university hospital and their renown hematology & oncology department. after additional testing, she met with dr.p who gave her the official diagnosis; a 10mm triple negative breast cancer tumor (tnbc) had developed in her left breast. in simplified non-medical terms, this type of cancer was known to be more aggressive, less responsive and have less treatment options than other forms of breast cancer.

the proposed plan of attack was straight forward; multiple rounds of chemotherapy to arrest the cancer's growth, followed by a lumpectomy to remove it. buoyed by the confidence and encouragement of dr.p and the other members of the university's team, Angela agreed and began her fight.

in true "i want what i want when i want it" style, Angela scheduled all of her chemo treatments, and subsequent follow-up appointments, around our upcoming trip to scotland. as she planned and looked forward to these trips months and years in advance, "there was no way in hell" cancer was going to stop her from going.

she also went to every appointment and treatment on her own.

no 'family'.

no husband.

just her.

when asked why she always went alone, Angela said that it was not out of some sense of bravery or stubbornness but rather that she "did not want anyone to have to experience" the sights and sounds of chemotherapy.

although she handled the chemo's well-known side effects exceptionally well, with fatigue only somewhat diminishing her drive, it was the hair loss that bothered her the most.

Angela loved her hair. it was one of her signatures and the envy of many. so it was upon our return home from scotland that she made a profound decision to do something that no one who knew her would have ever expected; she shaved her head.

it made perfect sense. with so little in her control, this was something that she could control. Angela was not going to let cancer take her hair. it was her hair and if it had to go, it would go by her hand. by her choosing.

and personally, i thought she looked more beautiful and even stronger without it.

ᚠ ᚾ

after a number of weeks her doctors informed her that they wanted to switch to a different type of chemotherapy, as it appeared that the cancer was continuing to grow despite their efforts.

a few more rounds using the different drugs, and the same result.

now the end of may, less than four months from the original discovery and diagnosis, Angela's doctors told her that based on the cancer's continued unresponsiveness to treatment that they now believed it was best to schedule her for a full mastectomy and flap reconstruction. the surgeries would take seven to eight hours, require a few days in the hospital, followed by six to eight weeks of recovery time. once recovered, they wanted to continue with a combination of radiation and an orally administered chemo until the end of the year.

knowing that her team of doctors were part of one of the best hospitals in the country, she agreed to their recommendations. chemotherapy treatments were discontinued to allow her body to get strong enough for the surgeries, which were scheduled for june twenty-first.

as the surgery date approached, Angela became understandably anxious. she knew what to expect based on what her doctors had told her and what she had researched online, however it was the unknown, the 'what ifs' that made the whole experience harder for her.

those uncertainties almost became too much for her to bare.

however on the day of the surgery, Angela was a rock.

i was not.

for anyone who has not had the misfortune of watching someone they care for lying in a hospital bed, the only words that can somewhat explain how it feels is 'sheer helplessness' and being 'trapped on an emotional rollercoaster'.

anger, fear, sadness, terror and everything in between. and expressing them will not ease the anxiety and pain your loved one is experiencing. nor will trying to 'act normal', which leaves you feeling callous and uncaring. a hellacious 'rock and a hard place'.

then, you stand there watching them be wheeled away.

knowing there is absolutely nothing you can do.

then you wait.

watching the clock.

battling your internal dialogue.

hour seven. "they should be done soon".

hour eight. "any minute now".

hour nine. "did something go wrong?"

and every second after that, "what the fuck!?!"

it was over twelve hours from the moment i watched them wheel my bride down a hallway to surgery to when i walked into her room. as expected, she was dazed from the anesthetic and pain medication, and visibly uncomfortable.

the following day Angela and i met with dr.p who informed us that although the tumor had grown to over 100mm (a ten fold increase), and that adjacent lymphs nodes had to be removed, the surgery was a success.

this was incredibly welcome news.

now all Angela needed to do was rest and recover.

easier said than done.

ʃ ⋈

as the hours continued to pass, Angela was in excruciating pain. every time she attempted to move she felt as if she was "being torn apart". more painful than her left breast area was her midsection where they had sourced the tissue for the reconstruction. the skin and tissues across her stomach and relocated belly button, were unwilling to stretch enough to allow her to sit or stand up straight, nor were they 'overly eager' to move in the other direction. this meant weeks in an arms elevated, bed-ridden, semi-crunched position with ever-present, excruciating pain. and yes, that was with her taking more than a one and a half dozen oxycontin a day.

once she was home, Angela's body began to recover. slowly. with each passing day, she experienced tiny bits of improvement. a little more mobility and a little bit less pain. eventually this gave her the freedom to slowly navigate our apartment on her own, albeit still hunched over.

it also gave her the shock of seeing her 'new body' in the mirror for the first time.

to be clear, Angela was not narcissistic or vain in anyway. she simply took pride in her appearance, whether it was wearing her favorite stella mccartney heels or a twenty year old concert t-shirt. remember, you can take the girl out of the fashion industry but you cannot take the fashion out of the girl.

beyond the expected bruising and swelling, it was the combination of the incisions around her misshapen breast and stomach, as well as the associated drainage tubes coming out of her body, that brought her to tears.

she knew the plastic surgeon who performed the reconstruction said it would take time for her body to 'settle in'. that they would be able to perform some 'fine-tuning' if needed after she had fully recovered. none of that prepared her for what she saw or how she felt.

"i look like frankenstein."

she was devastated.

but she persevered.

she continued with the prescribed chemo and radiation, as well as the painful physical therapy required due to the loss of arm and shoulder mobility (caused by the lymph node removal and associated axillary web syndrome aka cording).

her hair began to grow back.

she began to feel more like her old self again.

and she wanted to go away on a trip, "as soon as possible."

so true to form, Angela produced a fantastic three day getaway to one of our favorite destinations; las vegas. we ate. saw shows. walked the strip and celebrated the gift of time together.

with everything that had transpired over the past few months, we knew that being together and having our 'kids' (august aka augs and tomomi aka moo) was our everything.

more than ever we held on to what truly mattered

aria hotel las vegas

september 2016

.

5

upon our return from vegas, and Angela completing all of her post-op

appointments, we knew it was time to 'retire' to wine country. and having

researched our move to central california for over a year, we were really

excited to have found a house to rent in los alamos.

located about 50 miles north of santa barbara, los alamos was a

dramatic shift from the metropolis known as los angeles;

zero traffic lights.

a population of just over two thousand.

a town where people kept horses in their backyards.

a home that offered nightly sunsets overlooking a vineyard.

and the timing of everything worked out perfectly. we had a few weeks

of overlap between the expiration of our lease on the apartment downtown

and taking possession of our new place up north, which allowed for a very

low stress move. instead of the typical move-all-at-once madness, we were

able to drive small, nonessential stuff up with the cars, then the remaining

larger items in one last manageable truck load.

once settled, Angela began her search for work. initially she thought

that as she had no previous experience in the wine industry, securing a position may take some time. i reminded her that although she had never worked on a vineyard or in a wine shop before, she knew the product and process as well or better than many of the people we had encountered over the years (at the countless shops and wineries we had visited). plus, her overall professional skill set was second to none.

on this very rare occasion, i was right and she was wrong;

two interviews.

two immediate job offers.

Angela accepted a position in the tasting room at the rusack vineyard. not only did rusack produce some of her favorite wines, she loved her new boss, and the winery was located on one of the most beautiful properties in the santa ynez valley. so, unlike the countless hours of bumper-to-bumper traffic she had to deal with on the 10 freeway in los angeles, her new twenty minute 'commute' was filled with picturesque rolling hills and pastures of bisons, horses and sheep. it also didn't hurt that she got to spend her workdays with juju bee, the resident winery cat.

over the next few weeks and months, Angela quickly expanded her understanding of the business side of wine. it was amazing to hear her talk about her days at work. the new little vintner facts she had learnt, getting to be hands-on in the different aspects of the process and about the crazy, funny and heartwarming people she had met.

seeing her fulfill her dream of living and working in wine country was fantastic.

when we weren't working, Angela and i experienced central california much like we did the city. we would pick an area, such as morro bay, pismo beach or san luis obispo, and then plan our day around it. chilling at local hang-outs. shopping at local markets and stores. trying both new restaurants as well as old school, local institutions.

enjoying every moment we could together.

ᚠ ᛝ

Angela loved having things to look forward to; get-togethers, dinner and drinks, trips. anything that required planning and having fun. this was even more evident as she began "feeling like her old-self" again. the healthier she became, the more she wanted to plan and the more she wanted to do. and the upcoming new years was also a massive milestone for her.

it was not that she wanted to party in the traditional sense at some fancy event, but rather, to say good bye to a her last chemo pill and to a year that "really sucked balls."

for those who may be unaware, both the disease and the treatment of cancer dramatically weakens the immune system. something as simple as being in public places or eating certain foods pose a significant threat to the patient's health. for Angela this meant abstaining from one of her absolute favorite culinary joys: sushi.

so for her, there was no better way to celebrate surviving the worst year of her life than for us to return to her city, enjoy the day walking around historic olvera street and bustling downtown los angeles, all culminating in a beautiful sushi dinner.

to say that she enjoyed that day and that dinner would be a colossal understatement. the best description i can think of that will ring true to those who knew Angela best; she was 'eric cartman happy'.

eyes closed.

humongous smile.

clenched fists joyously vibrating in the air.

it was one of her happiest moments that i ever had the pleasure to witness.

ᚠ ᛈ

and with the start of the new year came incredible news. her first six month post-op follow-up tests showed no signs of cancer. she was given the 'all clear'.

Angela saw 2017 as a new beginning and an affirmation to enjoy as much life as she could. full steam ahead, she began planning her next "you don't age if you're out of town" birthday trip. and this time it was portugal.

why portugal? other than the sheer randomness of it, neither of us had ever been there and it was famous for its wine. however, choosing portugal also meant that we would postpone our long awaited trip to japan to the following year.

japan was a country that we both wanted to visit. a place that we had spoken about on our very first date, which made it the perfect destination for us to celebrate our tenth wedding anniversary in 2018.

professionally, Angela thrived. what started as part-time in the tasting room grew to becoming wine club manager and someone instrumental in planning all of rusack's events.

yet with so many positive happenings, the past remained ever-present.

Angela had a constant reminder of what she had endured. although the scars that marred her were not as pronounced or severe as they once were, they were still an enormous psychological burden on her being. something that she could not escape.

and once again, when faced with adversity, Angela's inner viking came through.

cancer may have scarred her body, but she was determined to reclaim it. she searched, found and scheduled an appointment with a tattoo artist to help her make that happen. and unlike so many other cancer survivors who found healing with feather or flower motifs, Angela was not about to go mainstream.

she wanted an all black, fine-line and pointillism based tattoo - a "crazy spirograph."

she transformed pain into power.

loss into strength.

and like countless times before, i was in awe.

we enjoyed our gift of now

museum of art, architecture and technology, portugal

march 2017

4

the spring of 2017 could not have been any more different that the year before. instead of a constant barrage of appointments and pain, Angela's days were spent helping people enjoy their experience at the winery and living a quiet country existence with "the kids" and i.

by the summer, she was feeling healthy again and with that improvement, the return of her energy and enthusiasm. and a longing.

she missed her 'family'.

she missed her city.

she wanted more.

she began asking people to visit. planning our trip to japan. doing fun stuff just for her. but unlike in the city where getting to something was as simple as my 'playing chauffeur' or calling an uber, Angela began spending hours driving and flying to different events. although she loved road trips, flying in planes, staying in hotels and everything that encompassed the travel experience, her body did not. come july, she began experiencing some severe back and hip pain.

august seventh was her second post-op follow up appointment with her doctors at the hospital in los angeles so Angela decided to make a day trip of it. she scheduled her appointment early so that she could spend some

time enjoying her city before making the three hour drive home.

that enjoyment never happened.

her mri results led to an immediate ct scan.

which led to an appointment with her oncologist the next morning.

all of this on the day that marked the twenty-fifth anniversary of her

mother's death.

ᚠ ᛞ

Angela and i met with dr.p the following morning.

when our worst fears were surpassed.

the cancer had returned, metastasizing in her left lung.

and it was terminal.

we were told that radiation and surgery were not viable options and

that a biopsy would be needed to help determine which type of

chemotherapy would be most effective to use. the goal was to hopefully

arrest the cancer's growth and help prolong Angela's life. she was told to

eat healthy, that they would do everything they could, and to remember her

death was not going to be immediate. she could still have years left to live.

we were gutted.

we needed to spend time together to talk and to decide what to do next.

we went to palisades park, a beautiful little area in santa monica over-looking the pacific and the pier. a place where we had played chess on many occasions.

we knew that regardless of the treatment's effectiveness, Angela needed to spend what time she had left in her city and with her 'family'. we immediate started planning our move back.

we also discussed whether or not she wanted to move forward with the proposed treatment plan, especially considering the chemo's lack of effectiveness the first go-around. and to ensure that she had absolutely no doubt, i told Angela that,

"this is your journey. your choice. and no matter what you want to do, i will support you. if you want to trust in their process, i'm there. if you want to say fuck it and go out on your shield, i'm there. i love you more than anything and i am all in."

꓿ ꓮ

it only took us a few days to find an apartment. it was close to her doctors, had directv so that Angela could "watch all the football" and ironically not far from where we first met. less than two weeks after that, we were completely settled back in los angeles.

and Angela was determined to enjoy it as much as possible.

we visited as many of our favorite spots as we could and even began a new tradition of trying new places that had been featured on various food shows. in between our time together, and her treatments, Angela also tried to spend as much time as she could with her 'family'. the tribe that she had built for herself over the years. the people who truly mattered to her.

unfortunately, her back and hip pain continued to worsen, becoming increasing debilitating. a slow walk became a labored shuffle. first she could move on her own, then only with the assistance of a cane.

Angela visited her general practitioner dr.b on two occasions about the pain. the first visit yielded a diagnosis of sciatica and provided Angela with a few prescriptions. the second included an x-ray, an increase in her medications and a referral to a back specialist with an appointment scheduled for mid october.

the increased medications yielded no relief. it had become so severe that during one chemotherapy appointment Angela was in such pain that, even with the assistance of multiple nurses, she was unable to step up a few inches onto a scale to be weighed.

combined with the side effects of the chemo, Angela spent much of september 'bed-ridden' on the couch. sitting was painful. standing excruciating. walking kept to an absolute minimum.

"one upside" she said, "moo and augs won't leave my side."

also keeping her company were some of her favorite shows; drag-race, golden girls, housewives, match game, project runway, pyramid, sex and the city, top chef and of course football!

f ⋈

there were twelve games scheduled for sunday october eighth, and although in a great deal of pain and experiencing new uti symptoms, Angela was determined to watch as much football as humanly possible. one of her 'sisters' was coming over. we were going to make brunch and enjoy a day jam-packed with the national football league.

then it happened.

while leaning against the kitchen counter, instructing me on how to prepare the tomatoes, Angela collapsed, nearly hitting the floor had her 'sister' not caught her.

she was in screaming agony.

we managed to get her back to the couch.

911 was called.

Angela was rushed to the university emergency room where, after an initial evaluation and pain medication, she was sent for multiple scans to determine what was going on.

a short while later dr.m came in and gave us the results.

"tumors have fractured your t6 vertebrae, and the broken pieces are impinging on your spinal column (in an area known to control bladder function causing the uti like symptoms). other tumors have fractured your right hip (causing the constant pain and contributing to the collapse). there are also tumors in your liver. we need to admit you immediately."

fuck.

we never thought it would happen like this

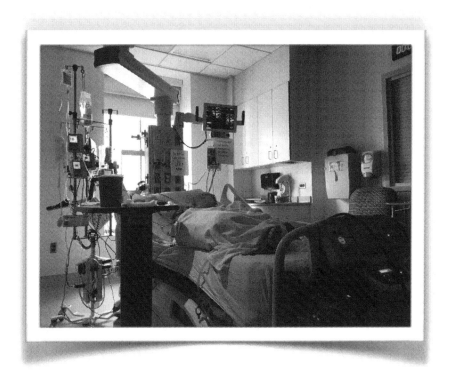

intensive care unit

october 2017

3

Angela was scheduled for two emergency surgeries.

first her spine.

neurosurgeon dr.l explained that they would remove the shattered vertebrae to alleviate the impingement on her spinal column, then fuse the spine together from above and below that area. beyond any 'worst case' complications, a lack of mobility and pain was to be expected, however those would improve over time and with rehabilitation.

after the surgery, Angela was placed in the intensive care unit.

she was in pain and she was scared.

this was not how she wanted her last days to be.

orthopedist dr.c was in charge of the hip surgery. he explained that, other than the fractures and tumors, the hip pain was being caused by the pressure of the femoral head impacting against the compromised pelvis. that is; whether Angela was sitting, standing or walking, the ball portion at the top of the thigh bone was in constant contact and pushing against her broken hip causing her incredible pain.

his proposed solution was to perform a femoral osteotomy; removal of not only the cancerous and fractured portion of the hip but also the femoral head itself. dr.c said that it was common procedure that would allow her to "be able to stand on it the next day" as the muscles and connective tissue surrounding the area would support her despite the various bones having been removed.

with everything that was going on, and even more swirling inside her head, Angela asked her primary oncologist, dr.p, to come visit her.

a familiar face.

a doctor who knew her.

a doctor she trusted.

they spoke about the surgery, but also of Angela's future. specifically, what Angela's goals were for when she left the hospital.

"i just want to be able to go out and spend time with my family."

ᚠ ᛝ

when they brought Angela back to the icu after the hip surgery, she was in indescribable pain and completely broken. and every movement caused by the team of nurses trying to get her reconnected to the various monitors and iv lines amplified it.

the coming days were even worse.

beyond the pain she continued to endure, which the doctors and nurses were having an incredibly difficult time managing, Angela had lost all control and nearly all sensation in her right leg. this complication meant that her room became a revolving door of orthopedic, neurology, nursing and palliative staff attempting to decipher what had gone wrong.

it was a week before she was 'well enough' to be moved out of icu and into a regular room. and with that move came different levels of care and concern.

even with Angela doing her best to manage her own medication schedule, consistent and timely delivery of her meds became a battle. and with each delay came the rapid return of white-knuckling pain, and further postponement of her next allowable dose.

the doctor's primary objective also seemed to shift. their focus appeared to become fixated on getting her "pain under control" enough so that she could be discharged to a different facility "better suited" for the recommended post-op rehab.

as the days ticked away, some sensation returned to Angela's right leg. however, control of it did not. nor were there any notable improvements in her pain. nor the timely delivery of her medications.

she simply got used to it.

i didn't.

i couldn't.

on many occasions i found myself trying to explain her entire medical history. her conditions and symptoms. how certain medications did not seem as effective as others. how the inconsistency of her pain meds was dramatically hurting her recovery. how "it's the rules" or "that's the system" were not an acceptable answers to the problems she was experiencing. how the "status quo" was clearly not working. asking when follow-up scans were planned to ascertain the status of the remaining cancer.

these questions yielded mixed results. the palliative team eventually modified her medication dosages and frequency for more consistent pain management. there were also multiple conversations with the head of the department dr.r.

first, he stated that there was no need to perform any further screening as "cancer doesn't work that fast". second, he informed me that my overall demeanor and the way in which i spoke with people made many of the hospital staff uncomfortable.

"i don't care. if they are uncomfortable, they should be asking themselves how would they react if it was their loved one in pain. what would they do in my situation?"

and to guarantee that there was no misunderstanding or uncertainty as to my position,

"i would burn the world if it would help her."

ᚠ ᛉ

after three weeks, two major surgeries, a somewhat effective pain medication schedule in place, and a constant barrage of "you will get better care and rehabilitation" Angela was released from the hospital and sent to a skilled nursing facility in santa monica.

if only that move had gone smoothly.

she was transferred to 'shady pines' around 4pm.

upon arrival she requested her next round of scheduled medications.

"we don't have them but they've been ordered from the pharmacy."

it was past midnight before Angela finally received her meds.

eight hours after arriving!

eight hours of needless suffering.

and no matter who i spoke with; whether it was administrative staff, doctors or nurses, from the university hospital she just left or those at 'shady pines', their responses were nothing more than a nonchalant 'sorry'.

sadly this first impression proved to be a just a glimpse into Angela's future.

although scheduled for some form of medication every hour or two, Angela almost never received her meds on time, other than a small handful of doses. not only did she need to constantly request her own medications, and follow up on those requests multiple times, dispensing was almost never recorded accurately which caused even greater confusion and delays. in addition, there were countless occasions when Angela was challenged by nurses as to whether or not she really needed any medication at all.

making matters even worse, her right thigh and hip continued to be a source of ever-increasing pain and swelling. this magnified her need for medication and diminished her ability to perform and benefit from any rehabilitation. when brought to the attention of the orthopedic doctors who performed the surgery, as well as the doctor at 'shady pines', all said that the swelling was "normal".

every day was another battle for Angela.

every day a heavier burden on her.

every moment excruciating.

beyond her off-property chemotherapy and immunotherapy treatments, Angela also had follow up appointments with neurology, oncology, orthopedics, and radiology back at the hospital. and as she could not get out of bed, or even sit in a wheelchair, every appointment required an ambulance for transportation.

every one of them meant her having to be lifted in and out of beds and gurneys. every one another 'jarring' ambulance ride. every one another pain-amplifying event.

more agony.

more incidents of mismanaged medication.

more doubt as to if anyone could or would actually help her.

we could not let this be her last stop

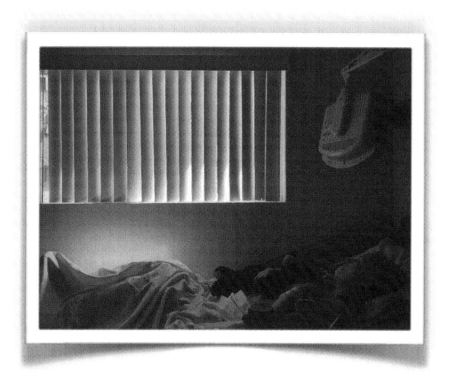

'shady pines' skilled nursing facility

november 2017

2

Angela had had enough.

after weeks of feeling "trapped in death's waiting room" she wanted to go home. she wanted to be with her "fur babies". to see and smell the outside world. to be in her own space and enjoy the company of her 'family'. she wanted to be in control again.

ᚠ ᛝ

november fifteenth was the happiest Angela had been in months.

she was away from doctors and nurses. away from iv bags and monitors. she was home for the first time in six weeks. and to this day, i am still surprised that moo survived being squeezed so lovingly hard, while auggie spun in endless circles like a complete lunatic.

we set Angela's hospital bed up in the living room so that she would have a view to both her left and right, with her large screen tv straight ahead. her medications were bedside, and with alarms set, she never missed a single dose. and wouldn't you know it, her pain levels dramatically reduced. she felt as good as she possible could and i slept on the couch five feet away for whenever she needed something.

the next day, follow-up ct and mri scans of her pelvis and spine were performed. the day after that dr.p emailed the results.

the lesions on her spine were still growing, as was the mass in her hip, which had doubled in size in less than a month. although the cancer was "growing very rapidly" dr.p wanted to discuss continuing with treatments.

Angela had other plans.

knowing how the chemo treatments made her feel, how much pain the transport to and from those appointments would cause, how fast the cancer had grown in the past even with chemo, and how there was no indication that she would benefit from any of that additional pain and suffering, Angela took control of her remaining time.

she decided to cease all further treatments.

she accepted that she was going to die.

and die soon.

F M

for the next few weeks, we found a rhythm.

Angela kept on top of her medication schedule, while i did my best to make sure that she had anything she needed or wanted. various hospice nurses came and went to make sure that her pain and symptoms were being managed as best as possible.

we spent time talking.

we spent time together.

and although her energy levels were decreasing, Angela kept her visitation schedule full.

she emailed and texted with her vast network of work friends and 'family' to coordinate visits morning, noon and night. she worked with their schedules, ensuring that everyone who came had her undivided attention. as with everything in her life before cancer, Angela took control of the situation and "produced the shit out of it".

we also started a new little evening ritual.

once her visitors had left, we would watch tv and enjoy some ice cream together. Angela would have either a small single serving cup of dulce de leche or vanilla with chocolate sauce on top, while i went a tad larger with a full pint of peanut butter cup ice cream. it was not quite the same as those times when we had enjoyed cones while strolling down state street in santa barbara or window shopping on upper street in islington, but it was still time together.

as the days continued to pass, Angela grew increasingly tired. there were moments where she would fall asleep mid-sentence. even times when she would fall asleep with a fork or spoon in her hand, which meant an occasional spill would have to be cleaned up.

there was one evening, with her bowl of ice cream still in her hand, Angela fell asleep. when i attempted to sneak the bowl away, i noticed that some of the chocolate sauce had spilt on the blanket near her right leg.

but when i started to clean the blanket i realized it wasn't chocolate.

it was blood.

Angela awoke to find herself lying in a three foot puddle of blood.

the hip incision, which had previously healed shut, had burst open under the unrelenting swelling she had been experiencing since her hip surgery in october.

hospice was immediately called and dispatched while we did our best to control the bleeding. unfortunately, the blood continued to flow. once the nurse arrived and assessed Angela's leg, it was decided that she needed to be transported to the emergency room.

in pain and terrified, Angela found herself yet again at the university hospital.

and once again, it was hours before she was comfortable.

it was not because the optimal dosages and medications to manage her pain were not known. those had been determined during her previous eight weeks of suffering. it was for no other reason than that the er doctors and nurses chose not to review her files, nor listen to the information both Angela and i attempted to provide.

when i asked "has the doctor reviewed her history" or informed them that a specific pain medication "did not work" i was dismissed. then ignored. then eventually threatened with removal from the hospital if i persisted.

it was at that moment that Angela gave me the 'stand-down' look, which i did reluctantly.

i could not risk her being alone.

later that night we were informed that the growth of the tumor in her hip, along with the associated blood flow and cellular ruptures, was the reason for the bleeding. we learned that this was "not surprising" or uncommon with that surgery, and that the recommended action was an embolization procedure to stop or at least restrict as many of the blood sources feeding the tumor as possible. we were also told that there was a good possibility that another bleeding event would occur, with additional embolizations being the only recourse.

now knowing what had caused the bleeding, and that it could happen again, Angela decided to have the embolization procedure.

one time.

she was tired.

and she never wanted to be in a hospital ever again.

ᚠ ᛗ

december tenth was the day Angela returned back home.

it was also the day that everything began to change dramatically.

her ability to swallow, her appetite, basic hand-eye coordination and muscle control all began dropping off. speaking clearly became a labor. typing on her phone virtually impossible. she no longer had any interest in having visitors.

the only thing trending up, was her pain.

taking into account Angela's full treatment history, the most recent hospitalization, as well as the trajectory of her condition, hospice made the recommendation to stop taking the more than three dozen daily pills, and switch to managing her pain with liquid morphine.

the liquid morphine worked exceptionally well at managing her pain, nearly eliminating it. however, it also led to Angela having a much more difficult time breathing as well as a slightly different reality. in exchange for relief, she experienced an ever increasing frequency of incoherent thoughts and vivid hallucinations.

the first time this happened i thought she was referring to something she had seen on tv with her "what's wrong with that lady's hair?" or "did you make the reservations?" however when she asked "what's with the union soldiers?" and "can you take care of the fish in the ceiling?" i knew that her brain was not firing the same. and however heartbreaking it was to 'play along' with her hallucinations, the only thing that mattered was that she was not in pain.

and then there were the occasional moments when Angela's personality came through, mixed with an equal portion of morphine.

one morning she asked me to get her "a bag to start packing up the art" so she could leave. another was when she channelled her best navin johnson impersonation, asking me to collect her items from around the apartment with "i need this, and this, and this".

ᚠ ᛗ

"husband?"

it was 12:30 in the morning.

"i want some orange juice."

"anything else?"

"no. just orange juice."

i threw on my shoes and walked to the nearest store. orange juice was an unusual request so i picked up a couple cans of dr pepper (her favorite) just in case she changed her mind.

upon my return, Angela had a few sips and then asked for her inhaler and a dose of morphine.

and then we talked

"i'm scared."

"i know babydoll."

"i love you."

"i love you too . . . more than anything . . . i don't want you to go . . .
but i don't want you to be in pain."

the next four gut-wrenching hours were a mix of heartfelt words, liquid
morphine, promises, tears, and even a few smart ass jokes. all interwoven
between Angela's gasping breathes.

at the worst moment in our lives, we talked like we always had;
honestly and hopelessly in love.

hand in hand

Angela continued to fight

we were still us, still together

until her gasps became one final soul-crushing gurgle

after that, we ceased to be we

she was gone

taken

stolen

forever

nine years and four months to the day we met

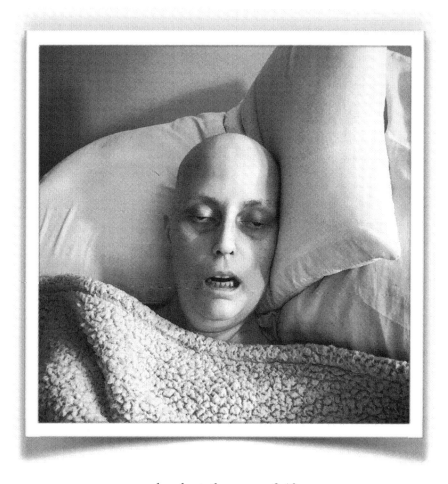

dead at the age of 43

december 22 2017

1

the void that Angela's death left was instantaneous.

immeasurable darkness

unfathomable rage

and within that void, was a tidal wave of emotions and an unrelenting

curse of hindsight. the manic 'what ifs' and the 'whys'. the mind-fuck of

constantly wondering how things could have been different 'had only' this

or that happened.

how things should have been.

as well as how things were.

i had just spent the best nine years and four months of my life with the

most amazing person i had ever met. i knew how lucky i was to have had

those last few months to be with her, no matter how horrendous they may

have been. time to tell her that she was my everything. and grateful in the

knowledge that it could have been much worse.

throughout her twenty-two month battle, especially during her last nine

weeks, we found ourselves sharing portions of her story with people. many

seemed to be trying to uncover how we 'kept it together'. how, even in the

worst time in our lives, we remained so in love.

for the most part, these interactions were positive, filled with concern and love. some were appropriate and thoughtful.

some were not.

ᚠ ᚼ

for those who didn't know us, one of the most common questions we were asked was "how did you meet?" this was almost always followed up with "how did you know?" or "what's your secret?" as so many viewed our relationship as a fairy tale.

people's reactions to our answers were always the same;

confusion and disbelief.

but our answers were simple.

we were simple.

we knew ourselves. who we were as individuals. what mattered to us and what didn't. and unlike so many who feel incomplete without a 'partner', we were confident and fulfilled in our own happiness. we did not require affirmation or validation from someone else to feel complete.

we never felt the need to ask anyone for permission to do something that made us happy. nor would we ever allow anyone to make us believe otherwise. to quote one of her favorite queens, "if you can't love yourself, how in the hell you gonna love somebody else?"

and we were honest.

completely honest with ourselves.

and each other.

we laid all of our cards on the table from the very beginning. for us, we did not try to 'be on our best behavior' or pretend. it was never about compromise. never about 'going along' with something we did not like or agree with.

it was about absolute, unwavering belief and support in each other in everything the other wanted. from what movie to see, to career choices, to even something as small as what restaurant we were going to enjoy that evening.

know and love yourself

never compromise what matters

always the truth

ᚠ ᛞ

Angela did not share her first diagnosis with many people. she kept it extremely private as she did not want people to 'act weird' around her or treat her like she was a 'make-a-wish kid'. all she ever wanted was for people to see her as they always had.

once the cancer was terminal, she let her entire world know.

some people reacted as she had hoped, continuing to treat her as 'their girl'. others reacted as she had feared.

people who we had thought would have been by her side were not. they became ghosts. no calls. no emails. no texts. nothing. Angela shrugged many of those off, but a few of them broke her heart. and then there were those who made every interaction about them, instead of her. who took the opportunity to try and unload their own guilt or shame for something that had happened in the past. and there were even a few who uttered such stupidity that they deserved a sledgehammer to their skull.

however, those disappointments were eclipsed by those who chose to step up.

those who were there for Angela day in and day out. constantly checking in on her, sending her messages, visiting her regularly, making sure she had everything she needed. without hesitation. without stipulation.

and there were even a few pleasant surprises.

people Angela had never expected to 'jump into the fire' for her. people that she had only known as acquaintances, friends of friends or through her professional network. people who made her feel truly special with their eagerness and willingness to go above and beyond.

of those who stepped up, who leaned in, not a single one was related to Angela in anyway. they were so much more than that.

they were her real 'family'.

a 'family' she had built over her twenty plus years in los angeles. the ones who had been there through thick and thin. who did anything and everything to make things easier for her. who showed her how much she meant to them. those who made her smile.

the ones who made Angela feel loved beyond belief.

never mistake relatives for family

and when shit goes down,

people either lean in or they lean out

ᚠ ᛗ

if there was one thing that Angela hated as much, or more, than her time in the hospital was being asked "how are you doing?" and "how are you feeling?"

she understood the intent behind these questions. Angela's disappointment and frustration came from the clear lack of empathy in asking her, the girl everyone went to for 'the truth whether they liked it or not', such a pedestrian question.

even though she was dying, Angela still expected authenticity.

no sugar coating.

no fake bullshit.

ever.

so when the 'greeting card' reactions started, her inner viking warrior came through. every 'get well', 'thoughts and prayers' and '#fuckcancer' that was meant to make her 'feel better' failed miserably.

these 'canned responses' just pissed her off.

and Angela let people know it.

i began reacting much the same way after she died.

every time i heard something like "i am sorry for your loss", "she is in a better place" or "i know it's hard" and "it takes time to heal", my first gut reaction was to respond with a "fuck you."

that usually got toned down to "fuck that."

to be clear, i did not lose my wife.

loss implies the ability to find. Angela was taken. and what little time she did have left to live her life on her terms was stolen by those sworn to help her. she did not 'pass'. it was not 'peaceful'. she died. painfully. and i cannot think of a better place for her to be than with her husband and the 'family' that loved her more than anything.

if i am wrong, prove it, otherwise sit down and shut the fuck up.

and please do not ever try to compare or think you know.

i have never had a child die and therefore cannot begin to understand how that might feel. it is incomprehensible. it is not inline with how things are supposed to be. neither is watching a 43 year old woman, living a good life, die. she was not old. she was not my grandparent, parent or elderly relative. not an acquaintance or an old classmate. she did not engage in dangerous or self-destructive behaviors. she never asked for it.

so unless you have watched the most important person in your world rot away in front of your eyes, listen to them describing the feeling of tumors growing inside them, hearing them say "i don't want to die" and have absolutely nothing to say in return that will bring them comfort, watch them as they struggle to breathe and see the fear swell in their eyes as they slowly suffocate to death, you haven't the faintest fucking idea of how i feel.

and as for the 'healing' people feel compelled to mention;

i was the one who administered Angela's liquid morphine at the end. i was the one medicating her to help take away her unthinkable pain. the same medication that took her mind. and her ability to breathe.

that is right. for those who are unaware liquid morphine, like many pain medications, is a respiratory depressant.

so what do you thinks happens when you take a girl with asthma and lung cancer and give her liquid morphine for unrelenting pain?

it kills her.

and i am the one who gave it to her.

which means i killed Angela.

i killed my wife.

think that thought rattling around in my fucking head gets any better with time?

leave your 'greeting card' bullshit at the door

be authentic, be honesty and bring unlimited quantities of

"i am sorry" and "i love you"

ᚠ ᛞ

Angela's diagnosis and treatment remains the primary source of painful hindsight. and the questions are endless;

why wasn't the tumor immediately removed from her breast when it was first discovered? why wasn't she scanned more frequently to accurately ascertain the tumor's growth? why wasn't an anti-cancer nutritional protocol prescribed? why not demand a patient be admitted for immediate diagnostics after collapsing during a treatment? how can a professional tell someone they may have a year or more to live, only to be hospitalized within weeks? why did it take a trip to the er to find out that the cancer had spread to her liver, hip and spine? why perform a surgery that could take six to twelve months to recover from when the patient may only have weeks or a few months to live? why, if a procedure is so common, do pillows have to be jerry-rigged in order to offer post-op comfort and support? why tell someone they will be able to stand the next day when in fact they become bedridden for the rest of their days? why not inform the patient that their leg might begin bleeding uncontrollably? why use "she could die" as the reason for not performing a more beneficial, albeit drastic procedure? why tell someone that "cancer doesn't spread that fast" when clearly it has? why discharge someone without their desperately needed medications being on-hand and ready for their arrival? why send a patient to a place where they receive lower quality care? why use drugs to control pain that aren't available outside the hospital? why not listen to the experience of the patient and advocate when it came to knowing what has and hasn't worked? why were the 'professionals' increasingly unsure as to what to do to help? and above all else, why not tell a terminal patient with a history of highly aggressive cancer that california, among other states and countries, offers a right-to-die option?

individually i am sure that some 'healthcare professional' would be happy to try and provide answers or explanations to any of the above questions. however, when viewed as a whole, it is clear to me that there is only one common denominator to them all; profit.

and whether they want to admit it or not, each and every person who benefits and or supports a system that gains from the suffering of others are nothing more than disease profiteers.

hippocratic oath?

hypocritical bullshit!

now, if after reading the above your instinctual response is to 'sue them', here are a few more questions to ponder;

did you know that 'pain and suffering' dies with the patient? that the courts do not value a person's 'quality of life'? that some medical malpractice cases can take years to complete? of those cases that people can afford to fight, the majority do not go their way? that the doctor, hospital and or insurance company are all allowed to sue you for their legal fees in defending against your lawsuit if you loose? and if by some chance you do happen to win, did you know that certain states have a limit to the compensation available? in the end, what will be left after that battle?

there is only one part of the medical system that works perfectly;

the part that protects itself.

knowing this, please take care of you and yours.

do your absolute best at minimizing illness and any associated risk factors. stay away from those things which you know bring you closer to relying on an industry that benefits more by keeping you sick. make your life about thriving, not just surviving. and if you do require medical attention of any kind, at any time, document everything.

dates, names, times, places. what was said and what was not said. take pictures of any and all medications, procedures, paperwork. audio or video record everything possible. ask questions. find out what all of your options are and all of the 'worst case scenarios'. then go over their answers with them. get second and third opinions. and always have someone with you at all times, especially if they have any advocacy and or first-hand patient experience.

remember; no matter how caring or pleasant a 'medical professional' may appear, they will undoubtedly be out of the picture the second you are no longer financially viable.

do not blindly follow the 'experts'

or accept their statements as absolute truth

question everything

ᚠ ᛞ

without question, had Angela been monitored more accurately, more frequently, things would have been different. had the cancer in her hip, liver, lungs or spine been discovered sooner, she would have lived her last few months differently.

she would have visited her favorite wineries again.

her favorite museums.

bought some silly expensive shit that made her smile.

spent time with her ‘family’.

in a pool.

watching football.

visited her ‘big kitties’ one last time.

she would have seen japan.

and she would have been free of regret.

had she been told that she would never walk again, or that she might wake up in a pool of her own blood, she would have told those doctors to shove that hip surgery up their ass and “just cut my fucking leg off”.

had she been informed of her right-to-die, she would not have chosen to suffer the agony of being house bound, then bedridden, multiple operations, months of unwarranted pain, or experienced four hours of slowly suffocating to death.

so, how did it go so wrong?

how were these mistakes allowed to happen?

why are the people we love forced to endure this kind of 'living hell'?

on december tenth 1948, the united nations declared thirty fundamental, and universally protected human rights. included in those rights are that "all human beings are born free and equal in dignity and rights" and that "no one shall be subjected to torture or to cruel, inhuman or degrading treatment or punishment."

yet, nearly seventy years later, those who are sick and suffering are not free. they are trapped in a system that benefits the longer they suffer. they are not provided full and accurate information to freely make educated decisions concerning their own dignified existence. that when their death is imminent, the system does not have the decency or humanity to grant them the right to peacefully end their hopeless struggle.

which begs the question;

if we truly are at liberty to live a life of our own choosing,

why are we not free to choose how that same life ends?

the only person who should control how you live

and how you die

is you

ᚠ ᛉ

once she was terminal, Angela became increasingly worried. not about herself, but about me.

about how, or if, i would be able to live without her.

and her concerns were valid.

whatever label you feel comfortable using, depression, malaise, or suicidal, the idea of killing myself was something that was not foreign to me. it was something i had considered for many years before meeting Angela, and continued to think about after we had met.

the only person i ever shared that with was her.

and what she said, and what she did not say, was what kept me from taking that step.

she was my purpose to continue living.

so once she came home after her time in the hospital and 'shady pines', we discussed dying. together. all four of us. august, tomomi, Angela and myself. our conversation was very pragmatic and felt as comfortable and normal as any other talk we had had over our nine plus years together. we had the means. the motivation. the opportunity. we knew our 'family' would understand, and we did not give a shit about those who would not.

but something did not feel right to me.

not because of some bullshit religious belief or societal view.

i simply told her "i'm not done yet."

however, those thoughts of ending my life are still in my mind. they have not left. they have grown louder, fueled by the ever-present, nearly all-consuming despair and heartbreak of not being with Angela. the replaying of her agony, of witnessing her soul slowly being crushed, of us holding hands as she died.

an emptiness that cannot be filled,

by anyone or anything.

ever.

however, these thoughts are no longer 'secret'. since Angela's death i have purposely shared my thoughts of self-determination, of suicide, with anyone who asks me "how are you doing?" or "how are you feeling?"

my reply is usually something like,

"there is not a day that has gone by since her death that i have not thought of putting a bullet in my head. but, i have promises to keep. i have to finish honoring her."

not surprisingly, nearly everyone who hears those words is shocked and taken aback. whether their shock is who is saying them, how frankly they are being said, or the fact that they were even said aloud, does not matter.

what matters is that not enough people talk about the concept of death, especially the possibility of killing themselves or someone they know killing themselves.

too many people respond with "i would never do that" or "not me". they pretend that they are immune to such 'weakness' as if it is somehow beneath them. that their 'faith' or 'moral compass' prevents such a thing from ever happening.

bullshit.

everyone is capable of killing, themselves or someone else.

it is just a matter of pressure and time.

those thoughts of ending it all never stop

there are no do-overs, no magic wands

but . . . there can be purpose

F M

Angela and i rarely spoke of our childhoods. for us, they were not a source of joyful or pleasant memories.

for me, i have very few vivid memories of being a kid. little more than flashes and snippets from over the years. however, there is one common thread that dominates those memories; a feeling of being lost, of not fitting in. that there was something wrong with me. regardless of how old i was, whether i was alone, with relatives or at school, something always felt off.

but i followed the program.

i graduated high school. i got a job.

dated a girl for three years. got married. bought a house.

i had attained everything that i had been told was 'important in life'. i had 'checked all the boxes' on the list of 'being an adult'. yet, i was immeasurably unhappy. completely unfulfilled. that feeling of being lost was still there. i had not outgrown it.

then illness and death impacted my life, in a positive way. it helped me realize that the feeling i had had my entire life, the feeling of being lost, was in fact the feeling of being purposeless. and that awareness, that wake up call, eventually led me to los angeles. it led me to Angela.

and from the moment we met, nothing else mattered more. my purpose was to do everything i could to make her happy. to show her how amazingly remarkable she was. to know how truly special she was.

and in the moment Angela died, all of her pain and suffering,

was not going to have been in vain.

it would become my purpose.

everyone and everything must have purpose

a purpose for being,

of doing

ſ ⋈

like everyone, Angela would have preferred certain parts of her life to
have been different. she would have avoided her less than 'brady bunch'
upbringing. skipped the experience of being made to feel worthless as a
child. having to watch her mother die of cancer when she was just a
teenager. or allowing anyone to treat her less than equal.

yet she accepted that those horrors helped shape her.

they helped create her and her mantra.

"i want what i want when i want it."

it was Angela's way of living life, and how she wanted others to live
their lives as well. she never saw any benefit to dwelling in the past or
spending time with people who dragged her down. no reason to work a job
where she was not appreciated or properly rewarded. no upside to being
absent from those experiences that brought her joy. she knew all too well
that life was fragile, and far too unpredictable to ever waste a moment.

now, think of all of the people and places that really matter to you. all
of the experiences and feelings that you hold dear. everyone and everything
that is truly important. now imagine that you have one hundred and thirty
seven days left to live.

the same number of days Angela had between her terminal diagnosis
and her death. you have just read how she spent hers.

how would you choose to spend yours?

your past is simply the path behind you

and tomorrow is never guaranteed

there is only now

ᚠ ᚾ

death.

there is no escape.

it is inevitable.

yet, it is almost never spoken about in everyday conversation. when it is, people try to find a specific cause or reason behind a person's death (such as illness, mental health, substance abuse, etc.) that does not apply to them, thereby somehow magically disqualifying them from the same fate. others attempt to find comfort in religious fables or spirituality. the rest simply avoid it all together.

but no matter how hard you ignore it, pray about it, or try and deny it

we

all

die

if the topic of death makes you uncomfortable, well, tough. quit acting like a spoiled little brat and face the reality of life.

remember the childhood fear you had of 'the monster' who lived in your closet or under your bed? remember what happened when you 'shined a light on it'? the fear went away. death is the same. so start talking.

be open about your feelings, hopes and wishes. the reasons you fear death. all of the 'what ifs', 'why did i', 'why did i not'. the 'could haves' and 'should haves'.

especially the one fear that haunts more people than any other;

regret.

it is only then that death can be viewed for what it truly is; an inspiration to live a life without regrets. a motivator to stop fucking around and wasting your time and energy on shit that does not matter. to stop passively watching your clock tick down.

to live a

"i want what i want when i want it"

life

the reaper is life's greatest teacher

and death its greatest lesson

reminding us to truly live

there were many people who were a part of Angela's life

as well as the journey she and i shared together.

and then there are those who were more . . .

to everyone at roseroom, for your amazing care and compassion

to angus and linda, for your unbelievable support

to trent, for the joy and happiness you brought to her

even in her darkest times

to my 'sisters' adrienne, ashley, cristina, deanne, frank, liz, nicole and

suzanne for being her 'family' when she needed you the most,

and for being mine now

to my 'brother' archie, the greatest father, friend, and

man i have ever known

thank you all from the bottom of my heart for everything you have done,

and continue to do

. . .

my friend

my partner

my love

. . .

words are incapable

of expressing who you were

and how much you meant to so many

. . .

always willing to stand for what was right when no one else would

willing to go to war for the family

you built over your lifetime

. . .

you made the dreams of a little Minnesota girl a reality

and did what you wanted

when you wanted

. . .

world travels and local dive bars

art, wine and top chef fine dining

plus a few industrial mosh pits for good measure

. . .

. . .

in a city and world that can crush the hopes and dreams

out of even the toughest, you were the epitome

of strength and thoughtfulness

. . .

you deserved more

than you ever asked for

and far more than i could have ever given

. . .

nothing and no one has meant more to me than you

moving forward

my sole mission is to honor you

. . .

my viking

my babydoll

my everything

. . .

rest in peace

. . .

(originally posted to instagram december 22, 2017)

Angela Dorian

march 29 1974 : december 22 2017

Made in the USA
Middletown, DE
18 March 2019